With Strong and Active Faith

Franklin

Delano

Roosevelt

I would like to thank my father, Blair Martin, for his help preparing this book, and my beloved wife, Chona, for her many months of patience. I would also like the thank John Whalen of Cider Mill Press for his support.

—Iain Martin

With Strong and Active Faith

THE WISDOM OF FRANKLIN DELANO ROOSEVELT

By Iain C. Martin

CIDER MILL PRESS

BOOK PUBLISHERS

Kennebunkport, Maine

13-Digit ISBN: 978-1-60433-136-3

This book may be ordered by mail from the publisher. Please include $3.50 for postage and handling. Please support your local bookseller first!

Books published by Cider Mill Press Book Publishers are available at special discounts for bulk purchases in the United States by corporations, institutions, and other organizations. For more information, please contact the publisher.

Cider Mill Press Book Publishers
"Where good books are ready for press"
12 Port Farm Road
Kennebunkport, Maine 04046
Visit us on the Web!
www.cidermillpress.com

Design by Ponderosa Pine Design, Vicky Vaughn Shea

Typography: Alons Antique, Arno Pro, Baskerville, Bickham Script, Excelsior, Freehand 521, Gill Sans, Myriad, Olduvai, P22 Declaration, Snell Roundhand Script

All photos are courtesy of the Franklin Roosevelt Library, except for the following:
p. 38 Campobello by Jim Loftus.
p. 64. Migrant Mother by Dorothy Lange, Library of Congress.
p. 71. Breadline, ©Shutterstock.com/4736202690
p. 73. Springwood Estate by Peter K. Law.
p. 82. Child labor, cranberry bog, Burlington County, New Jersey, National Archives.
p. 113. U.S.S. *Arizona*, U.S. Naval Historical Foundation
p. 158. Thomas D. McAvoy
p. 163. FDR Memorial, ©Shutterstock.com/nfsphoto
p. 164. FDR Memorial by Tony Fischer.
p. 167. Roosevelt grave site at Hyde Park by Iain Martin

(Special thanks to Mark Renovitch, Alycia Vivona, and Virginia Lewick at the FDR Library for their valuable assistance.)

Printed in the United States of America

1 2 3 4 5 6 7 8 9 0

First Edition

Table of Contents

Franklin Delano Roosevelt, 1917

Preface

Of all the great leaders throughout history, none has fascinated me more than Franklin Delano Roosevelt. Born to privilege and wealth, he chose to enter public service and champion those with no political voice. Crippled by polio, he persevered to achieve his lifelong goal of becoming president of the United States. He was destined to lead not only his country through the Great Depression but to victory in World War II. Franklin Roosevelt became the icon of hope for freedom-loving people across the embattled world as they resisted the onslaught of fascism.

As a young boy, I saw this firsthand when my parents, both survivors of the Battle of Britain, showed me their hiding places where as children they took shelter from German bombs. I have seen the beaches at Dunkirk, where the British army evacuated under fire in the early summer of 1940, using any craft that would make it across the English Channel. England was nearly defenseless against a Nazi invasion. It was Franklin Roosevelt, urged by Winston Churchill, who risked his presidency to send the weapons, supplies, and most importantly, the ships that saved Britain. It dawned on me at an early age that history was more than great stories in old books—it was personal.

This book offers a collection of Franklin Roosevelt's finest words taken from his speeches, letters, and conversations. It does not intend to debate or analyze politics or history. Yet as we stand near a new waypoint on the future direction of the United States, it is interesting to look back at Roosevelt's era and see the issues faced then were not all that different from the issues we face today. No president has been loved or reviled as much as Franklin Roosevelt. Scorned by conservatives as the creator

> "Let me assert my firm belief that the only thing we have to fear is fear itself"

of big government and the welfare state, he is equally lauded by those who believe in the government's social duty to oversee the well being of the people. We tend to forget the great dangers of Roosevelt's era—that overcoming the Depression and victory in the Second World War were not predestined events. At the time of his passing in April 1945, friends and foes alike recognized the greatness of Roosevelt's political skills, his ability to inspire, and his vision for the future of democracy around the world. We are living out his vision of freedom today. Agree or disagree with his politics, Franklin Roosevelt was a great American who loved his country and especially the people of his country in whose service he devoted his life.

Franklin with his son James in Washington, D.C., in 1934.

The Happy Warrior

In modern times, there is only one president to whom all the rest are compared—Franklin Delano Roosevelt. Elected to office four times, he was perhaps loved and hated as no other American president before or since. A son of the Gilded Age and born into the wealthiest class of American families, he would champion the rights of working classes and the "forgotten man," garnering the hatred of his political enemies as "that man in the White House" and "a traitor to his class." Taking office at a convergence of natural and economic disasters in 1933, Franklin devoted himself not only to the restoration of confidence in American institutions but to the dignity of the American spirit. For millions, he became the chosen savior. His politics of the New Deal for the American people redefined the federal government's responsibility to care for those in distress as a social duty. An entire generation of Americans looked to

FDR (as he came to be known) for leadership as the nation faced its darkest times through the Great Depression and into World War II. By the time of his death on April 12, 1945, FDR had not only saved democracy, he also placed the United States at the apex of international power and prestige.

A Leader Through and Through

Franklin Roosevelt is best remembered for his serene confidence and vitality, the very image of an American president, with warmth of heart, magnificent smile, great humor, and obvious delight in people. His clear, ringing voice crossed the nation by radio moments after taking the oath of office on March 4, 1933, in his first inaugural address, when he uttered the famous words: "First of all, let me assert my firm belief that the only thing we have to fear is fear itself." Recognizing the desperate need for action, he announced his intention to ask Congress for "broad executive power to wage a war against the emergency, as great as the power that would be given to me if we were in fact invaded by a foreign foe." FDR knew the consequences of failing to seize the day. Just after the ceremony, a visitor told him, "Mr. President, if your program succeeds, you'll be the greatest

"We do not distrust the future of essential democracy. The people of the United States have not failed."

president in American history." Roosevelt responded, "If it fails, I'll be the last one."

It was a pivotal moment in the nation's history. The stock market crash of 1929 sent the United States into the uncharted waters of a deep economic depression. As FDR assumed the presidency, the country edged ever closer to the abyss. Nearly a third of the labor force was unemployed, factory production was down by 50 percent, and agriculture could find no markets for their crops as prices fell by 60 percent. Investments were down by an incredible

President-elect Franklin Roosevelt and President Herbert Hoover on the way to the Inaugural ceremonies, March 4, 1933.

90 percent. Thousands were losing their homes and farms every week, leaving two million Americans homeless by 1933. Millions of people had seen their life savings vanish overnight as banks failed. The day before Roosevelt's inauguration, the New York Stock Exchange suspended trading indefinitely. On March 4, 1933, banks in thirty-four states had been ordered to close on holiday by state governments to prevent chaos. The nation was desperate for leadership, action, and hope. As historian Arthur M. Schlesinger Jr. noted, "It was now not just a

A bread line in New York City in 1932.

matter of staving off hunger. It was a matter of seeing whether a representative democracy could conquer economic collapse. It was a matter of staving off violence, even (at least some so thought) revolution."

FDR's response to the crisis became the legendary hundred days in which he sent Congress a record number of bills focused on immediate relief, all of which passed in record time. The day after he took office, Congress approved FDR's Emergency Banking Act, declaring a national bank holiday to meet the crisis head-on by issuing new currency and reorganizing federal support. Banks reopened after FDR spoke to the nation by radio in his first "fireside chat" on the evening of March 12. Across the nation, people gathered around to hear the new president address them directly. From the airwaves came the calm, confident voice speaking to them in clear and simple terms on his first actions as president. "I can assure you," Franklin told listeners, "that it is safer to keep your money in a reopened bank than under the mattress." The next day, when the first banks reopened, the majority of people began depositing their savings again, and catastrophe was averted.

In the months that followed came a windfall of new legislative acts, federal agencies, and executive orders to provide relief for the unemployed and tackle the causes of the Depression in an alphabet soup of new programs: the Federal Deposit Insurance Corporation (FDIC), Civilian Conservation Corps (CCC), and the Agricultural Adjustment Administration (AAA). These were soon followed by the National Industrial Recovery Act (NIRA), Public Works Administration (PWA), and Tennessee Valley Authority (TVA). Roosevelt also began the repeal of prohibition by approving the Cullen-Harrison Act on March 23, allowing the sale of beer and light wines, commenting after signing the amendment, "I think this would be a good time for a beer."

> "I think this would be a good time for a beer."

Franklin's remark was a sign of the times, ushering in a new era of change and hope for the future. When the hundred days were over, Roosevelt had signed fifteen major bills into law, saving the financial system and putting hundreds of thousands of people back to work. "We have had our revolution," one magazine reported, "and we like it." Although tough days remained ahead, the nation had its leader, the chosen savior who spoke to them as friends and who, with his ebullient good nature and supreme confidence in himself and his country, would lead the people onward.

Franklin Roosevelt throwing the first ball at a game in Washington, D.C., on April 24, 1934.

Roosevelt's strength of character came from a profound Christian faith and a family upbringing that gave him great confidence in his own abilities, in the good nature of others, and the upward course of human events. Any challenge to the American people could be solved through hard work, adaptability, and faith in the Almighty.

Franklin was also greatly affected by his long struggle to overcome paralysis. Since the age of thirty-nine, he had lost the use of his legs from polio. FDR's ascendancy to the White House is a story of courage, perseverance, and will to overcome the physical and mental barriers placed in his way by fate. Yet his trials to regain the ability to walk put him in touch with everyday Americans as they faced their own struggles against poverty. Although few Americans at the time knew the extent of his disability, they sensed Roosevelt understood hardship and suffering. People knew he believed in them, and they loved him for it. That faith was rewarded with the loyalty of a people starved for leadership. As one G.I. put it, "He became the commander in chief of our generation."

During the second half of his presidency, Roosevelt would also lead the United States and its allies to victory in the Second World War. The Great Depression had been a worldwide catastrophe that allowed fascist governments to seize control of Germany, Italy, and Japan. By forming the Tripartite Pact in September 1940, the three Axis governments directly challenged the supremacy of the remaining democracies. Recognizing that a new European conflict was likely, Roosevelt began careful and deliberate re-armament of a nation unprepared for war. He would risk his presidency in the defense of Great Britain in 1940 by challenging the neutrality laws to provide weapons and support for his besieged ally against the Nazis. The day after the United States was directly attacked by Japan on December 7, 1941, at Pearl Harbor, Roosevelt's "day of infamy" speech would rally the nation to victory. Not losing sight of his vision for world peace, FDR organized the United Nations, which was founded soon after his death on October 24, 1945, with Eleanor Roosevelt as the first appointed delegate for the United States.

Born with a Silver Spoon

The man who would one day champion the common man arrived into the world to the most privileged of upbringings. Franklin Delano Roosevelt was born on January 30, 1882, at his father's Springwood estate in Hyde Park, New York. James Roosevelt was a sporting country squire of Dutch ancestry, a fourth-generation descendant of Nicholas Roosevelt, whose two sons Johannes and Jacobus founded the Roosevelt clans at Oyster Bay and Hyde Park in the early eighteenth century. James's mother, Mary Rebecca Aspinwall, was a first cousin of Elizabeth Monroe, wife of the fifth U.S. President, James Monroe. One of his ancestors was John Lothropp, also an ancestor of Joseph Smith, Jr., and Benedict Arnold. James's wealth came from interests in coal and railroads, in addition to farming his Hyde Park estate. His mother, Sara, was one of five daughters of Warren Delano II, an aristocrat related to four of the original *Mayflower* passengers. Warren had made a vast fortune in the China trade. James had been a widower for four years when he first met his distant cousin, Sara Delano, at the home of Theodore Roosevelt in 1880. He was fifty-two years old and had a son, Rosy, by his first marriage. Sara was exactly half that age. Their combined wealth and family names placed them at the apex of society.

Delivering Franklin had been a dangerous ordeal for Sara, and doctors advised her not to have more children. Named by his mother after her favorite uncle, young Franklin enjoyed a

Franklin D. Roosevelt and James Roosevelt in Hyde Park, New York, 1891.

childhood at Hyde Park with the full devotion of two adoring parents. James had a warm heart and quiet sense of fun, and both traits were inherited by Franklin. He taught his son to ride horses, shoot, swim, and most important, to sail, first on the Hudson and later on the Bay of Fundy off Campobello Island in New Brunswick where the family owned a summer home. James was also a strong role model as vestryman of the St. James Episcopal Church of Hyde Park, a position Franklin would also hold one day. By all accounts, James was a loving and gentle father to Franklin.

As Sara's only child, Franklin would benefit from (and

THE YOUNG FRANKLIN ROOSEVELT

TOP: **Franklin, age three, in 1885**

MIDDLE: **James Roosevelt with son Franklin in 1887**

BOTTOM: **Sara Roosevelt and son Franklin in 1887**

TOP: **Franklin's portrait in 1889**

MIDDLE: **Franklin, age 12, in 1895**

BOTTOM LEFT: **Franklin in 1897**

BOTTOM RIGHT: **Franklin with his parents in 1899**

endure) her single-minded devotion throughout his life. Learning to care for him as an infant, Sara took on the tasks of motherhood without the assistance of a nursemaid. "At the very outset, he was plump, pink, and nice," his mother said. "I used to love to bathe and dress him. He looked very sweet, his little blonde curls bobbing as he ran as fast as he could whenever he thought I had designs on combing them." She delighted in dressing him in kilts and sailor suits to match the Little Lord Fauntleroy style of the day. Such was her dedication that Franklin was eight before he was allowed to bathe himself. Sara was the disciplinarian and arranged Franklin's daily activities by the hour. He was tutored at home and rarely allowed to play with anyone except his cousins or children from neighboring estates. It was a perfect little heaven for a small boy to grow up in, far removed from the harsh realities of the outside world. Franklin later reminisced, "In thinking back to my earliest days, I am impressed by the peacefulness and regularity of things both in respect to place and people."

Franklin Roosevelt, age three, in 1885.

At age fourteen, Franklin left Hyde Park to attend boarding school at Groton. There he came under the tutelage of

Headmaster Endicott Peabody, who preached the duty of Christians to help the less fortunate and urged his students to enter public service. His influence on Franklin ran deep. Not only did Franklin ask him to officiate at his wedding in 1905, he would preside over three of Roosevelt's inaugural services. At Franklin's fourth inaugural speech, three months after his mentor's passing, he referred to Peabody directly, reminding Americans "the trend of civilization itself is forever upward."

Franklin's years at Groton, however, were not happy ones. Too slight of build and inexperienced in team sports, he did not fit in well with the other boys. The only prestige Roosevelt could claim was that he was a fifth cousin of Theodore Roosevelt, the newly appointed assistant secretary of the navy. Theodore visited Groton during Franklin's first year, pronouncing, "If a man has courage, goodness, and brains, no limit can be placed on the greatness of the work he may accomplish. He is the man needed in politics today . . ." Theodore became Franklin's idol—the ideal example of a gentleman in government, and Franklin even adopted Theodore's gold-rimmed pince-nez glasses in 1899. By his graduation in 1900, Groton instilled in Franklin a desire to follow in Teddy's footsteps and enter public service, but he also adopted a keen awareness that he was not one of the boys.

Franklin had always loved the sea and wished to enter the U.S. Naval Academy, but as the Roosevelt's only son, he accepted his parents' wishes for him to attend Harvard

University. Franklin was keen to win recognition from his peers and was elected editor-in-chief of the college newspaper, *The Crimson*, his senior year. His college experience was slighted, however, by his failure to gain admission to the Porcellian, Harvard's most exclusive club. Voting in secret, one of the members had black-balled Franklin's admission. It was an insult FDR later claimed was the greatest disappointment of his early life. Many of those same club members would be stunned one day to see Franklin elected president. They would not be the last people to underestimate him.

Franklin Meets Eleanor

On December 8, 1900, as Franklin attended his first semester at Harvard, his beloved seventy-two-year-old father passed away from heart failure. In mourning, Sara moved to an apartment near Franklin's. A family friend wrote, "She would not let her son call his soul his own." Such was the intensity of Sara's dominance that Franklin became an expert in concealing his true thoughts and intentions, a trait that later served him well in politics. A year later, Franklin fell in love with Eleanor Roosevelt, a fifth cousin once removed. They had known each other as children, but in 1902 at age seventeen, she had just returned from England, and Franklin, then twenty, was attending law school at Columbia University. A few months later on New Year's Day, after a White House reception and dinner with Eleanor's uncle, President Theodore Roosevelt,

Franklin and Eleanor Roosevelt at Campobello, August 1904.

Franklin began to court Eleanor in earnest. Until Franklin told Sara of his intention to marry, he and Eleanor shrouded their courtship in secrecy.

Eleanor was the daughter of Elliot Roosevelt, brother to Theodore Roosevelt, and Anna Hall Roosevelt, one of the most beautiful women in New York society. Three years younger than Franklin, she had been educated at Allenswood Academy near London, an elite finishing school for upper-class women under the headmistress Marie Souvestre. Unlike Franklin's idyllic early life, Eleanor's had been a series of tragedies. At age eight, she lost her mother to diphtheria, a disease that would also claim the life of her brother Elliott Jr. Two years later, her beloved father died from a lifelong addiction to

Elliott Roosevelt, brother of Theodore Roosevelt, with his daughter Eleanor, July 1889.

alcohol. She would forever consider herself "Little Nell," the pet name her father had given her, after the sweet, shamefully victimized heroine of Charles Dickens's *The Old Curiosity Shop*. Raised from early adolescence by her maternal grandmother, Mary Ludlow Hall, Eleanor was painfully shy and withdrawn. It was perhaps this serious nature of her character that drew Franklin to her.

Eleanor saw underneath the bright charm and laughter of Franklin's outward appearance. Her cousins thought of Franklin as a "feather duster," someone who floats through a life of shallow character. Yet Eleanor knew there was also a depth to Franklin that most had not yet recognized. Curtis Roosevelt, Franklin and Eleanor's oldest grandson, noted, "I think FDR was very much attracted to my grandmother because they were two lonely people, two people who were not totally satisfied with the standards and ideals of their upper-class group. And I think the two of them looked at each other and knew that they could draw strength from each other."

Sara opposed the match on the grounds that Franklin was too young at twenty-one and still attending law school with no means of support other than his trust fund. She made the couple keep the engagement secret for a year until it was announced on December 1, 1904. Franklin wrote to his mother apologizing for keeping the relationship a secret from her: "Dearest Mama, I know what pain I must have caused you, and you know I wouldn't do it if I really could have helped it, but I know my mind and I'm the happiest man just now in the world."

Franklin and Eleanor were married on March 17, 1905, in the twin, interconnecting brownstone houses of Eleanor's cousin, Mrs. Henry Parish, Jr., and Mrs. Parish's mother, Mrs. Livingston Ludlow. They lived at numbers six and eight, on East 76th Street in New York, opening the doors between living rooms for the ceremony with an altar set up before the fireplace. The President of the United States arrived to give away the bride, who was his favorite niece. Reverend Endicott Peabody was at hand to perform the service. Afterwards, Teddy Roosevelt shook hands with the groom and said, "Well, Franklin, there is nothing like keeping the name in the family."

That summer, the couple took a leisurely three-month honeymoon on a grand tour of Europe. Eleanor returned pregnant with their first child. Anna Eleanor Roosevelt was born on May 3, 1906, followed by James Roosevelt on December 23, 1907, and Franklin Delano Roosevelt, Jr., on March 3, 1909. Sara had leased a home for them at 125 East 36th Street, three blocks from her own at 200 Madison Avenue. She also purchased a lot at East 65th Street and had twin six-story houses built by the noted architect Charles A. Platt with interconnecting sliding doors and a shared vestibule. When they were completed in 1908, Franklin and Eleanor moved into number forty-nine with Sara habitating the adjoining number forty-seven. Both homes were completely furnished, staffed, and managed by Sara, who also kept title to both.

The following year, in the summer of 1909, Sara purchased a belated wedding gift for Franklin and Eleanor—a rambling thirty-four room wooden cottage next to her own summer home on Campobello Island just off the coast of Maine. The family would enjoy some of their happiest days there. It was at Campobello that Eleanor could enjoy a home she would call her own, and Franklin would spend countless hours teaching his children to sail, hike the shoreline,

> "We spent so little time alone with our parents that those times are remembered and treasured, as though gifts from the gods."
>
> —James Roosevelt

and swim. James Roosevelt wrote later, "We spent so little time alone with our parents that those times are remembered and treasured, as though gifts from the gods."

That fall, the Roosevelts suffered the first serious tragedy of their married lives when Franklin Jr. fell ill with pneumonia and passed away on November 7, 1909. He was just seven months old. It was a crushing loss for both parents, especially Eleanor, who blamed herself for his death. He was "the biggest and most beautiful of all the babies," as she remembered him. They were only consoled by the birth of Elliott on September 23, 1910.

Early Political Life

That year proved a turning point in Franklin's career. He had left Columbia University in 1907 after passing the New York Bar exam to take a job as a law clerk at the Wall Street firm of Carter Ledyard & Milburn. Much like his studies, Franklin found the practice of law to be uninteresting. It was in these first working years that he revealed his intentions to enter public service. A fellow clerk at the firm, Grenville Clark, recalled, "He said he intended to enter political life as soon as he could, with a view to becoming president. He said that modestly enough but very definitely, and he laid out a definite plan." That plan was to follow in Teddy Roosevelt's footsteps—assistant secretary of the navy, governor of New York, and president of the United States.

Roosevelt, right, campaigning with Governor James Cox of Ohio in 1920.

His first chance to enter politics came in the fall of 1910 when the leaders of the Democratic Party from Poughkeepsie asked him to run for the state legislature. With his mother covering expenses, Franklin hired a gaudy fire-engine-red Maxwell touring car nicknamed "The Red Peril" and barnstormed the state alongside Richard Connell, who was running for a seat in the U.S. House of Representatives. Driving over two thousand miles around the district near Hyde Park, Franklin met every Republican farmer he could. The comic highlight of the campaign occurred one afternoon when the car pulled up to a small-town saloon. Franklin breezed inside and bought everyone a round of drinks, only to discover they were in Sharon, Connecticut!

When the votes were tallied, Franklin won a decisive victory as part of a Democratic landslide that year. In Albany, the family wealth allowed him to devote his full attention to politics. He immediately leapt into the fire by leading a revolt against the New York political machine from Tammany Hall, under the leadership of the vaunted "Big Tim" Sullivan. At the time, state senators were chosen by the legislature. Franklin rallied a group of rebels to block the nomination of Tammany Hall's candidate, William F. Sheehan. The effort made Franklin many enemies as his peers came to see him as a rich Harvard upstart, yet it gained him national attention in the media.

During the Sheehan fight at the state senate, Franklin also met a second-string reporter for the *New York Herald* named Louis Howe. A gnome of a man, Howe "had more skills at his fingertips than half a dozen other men combined," Elliott recalled. He could write anything from a poem to a fast-breaking news story. He had a solid reputation with his editors for tireless research and astute political analysis, which made him an uncannily accurate forecaster of election results. For his part, Howe was greatly impressed by the young Roosevelt. "Almost at that first meeting," he later said, "I made up my mind that nothing but an accident could keep him from becoming president."

> "Father in those days was cocky, impatient, and ambitious ..."
>
> —James Roosevelt

Franklin's career next took him to Washington, D.C., in the spring of 1913 as the Wilson Administration took office. Wilson's appointed naval secretary and an admirer of Franklin asked him to serve as his assistant. It was a moment Franklin had waited for all his life. Two days after taking the oath of office, Daniels was out of Washington and Franklin told reporters, "There's a Roosevelt on the job today. You remember what happened the last time a Roosevelt occupied a similar position?" He was thirty-one years old, the youngest man to ever hold that appointment in the navy's history. James Roosevelt, FDR's eldest son, later wrote, "Father in those days was cocky, impatient, and ambitious, and it is a miracle that Josephus, the sage Tar Heel editor, liked and tolerated him as much as he did." Yet his seven years in office helped prepare him for the White House—a hands-on education in the arts of political patronage and diplomacy, working with unions and working men and learning the ways of federal appropriations. By the time he became president in 1933, he knew more about the navy and naval strategy than any president before him.

Love and War

Two more sons arrived for Franklin and Eleanor during these years—Franklin Delano Roosevelt, Jr., on August 17, 1914, and John Aspinwall Roosevelt on March 13, 1916. Yet these would prove to be some of the most difficult times for their marriage. Cracks had formed between the couple as Eleanor did not enjoy the Washington scene in which she had many official social duties that came with her husband's position. She was also pregnant with her fifth child, which made things all the more difficult. To help with the workload, she hired a social secretary, Lucy Page Mercer. Elliott described her as

Franklin touring the Philadelphia Navy Yard in October 1917.

"twenty-three years old, with a rich contralto voice, femininely gentle, where Mother had something of a schoolmarm's air about her, outgoing where Mother was an introvert."

Lucy's mother, Minnie Tunis, was a divorced aristocratic heiress who remarried Carroll Mercer, a relative of Charles Carroll, a signer of the Declaration of Independence. His family name, coupled with Minnie's wealth, put them at the top of society. Although her family had lost their fortunes through circumstance, Lucy was in the social registry for New York and Washington—"a lady to her fingertips," as Elliott recalled. A lifelong Washington resident, Lucy was the perfect secretary to help Eleanor. As Eleanor often spent summers at the Campobello and New York homes, Lucy would stay to attend to her business and accompany Franklin to Washington functions and social gatherings.

Franklin and Lucy soon became the subject of Washington gossip. Alice Roosevelt Longworth, Teddy Roosevelt's spitfire daughter, encouraged the situation by having Franklin and Lucy to dinner when Eleanor was out of town. Alice later said, "It was good for Franklin. He deserved a good time. He was married to Eleanor." Elliott later wrote that, "Lucy had the same brand of charm as Father, and there was a hint of fire in her warm, dark eyes. In the new circumstances of Father's life at home, I see it as inevitable that they were irresistibly attracted to each other."

Eleanor wrote about the summer of 1916 in her memoir:

"From a life centered entirely in my family, I became conscious that there was a sense of impending disaster hanging over all of us." The casual reader may infer Eleanor spoke of the impending war with Germany, yet Elliott and James both agree she meant the coming reckoning with Franklin over his affair with Lucy. The following August, tensions neared a breaking point when Eleanor wrote Franklin from Campobello, "Remember, I count on seeing you on the 26th. My threat was no idle one." Elliott later stated in his own memoir she had threatened Franklin with divorce.

Portrait of Lucy Mercer Rutherfurd, ca. 1937.

Franklin had been keen to resign his position and join the navy as war loomed closer towards the American declaration of war in April 1917. President Wilson reminded Franklin he had much more power and influence over events where he was. "Tell the young man to stay where he is," he instructed Daniels. Sent to Europe more than a year later at the end of World War I to oversee naval business, Roosevelt crossed on the destroyer U.S.S. *Dyer* and spent weeks touring the front and meeting heads of state. He witnessed the aftermath at Belleau Wood, where only weeks earlier the U.S. Marines had fought a desperate battle.

Franklin inspecting the battlefields of the western front in 1919.

The detritus of war, the shallow graves where Americans had fallen, and the shattered landscape affected him deeply. Even if he had missed serving in combat, he at least witnessed war's true nature.

On the return voyage aboard the U.S.S. *Leviathan*, Franklin fell ill with the influenza epidemic that eventually claimed the lives of many of the ship's complement before it arrived in New York on September 19, 1918. Franklin, semiconscious, was carried off the ship and moved to Sarah's home on East 65th Street. Unpacking his luggage, Eleanor discovered a packet of love letters between Franklin and Lucy, proving her worst fears. "The bottom dropped out of my world," she later remembered. "I faced myself, my surroundings, my world, honestly for the first time."

Eleanor offered Franklin a divorce, which at first he may have wanted to accept. Sara and Louis Howe brought the couple back to reality. Sara made it clear to Franklin that if he left Eleanor, she would withdraw her financial support and the inheritance of the family home at Hyde Park. Louis got through to his best friend that if he became a divorced man, not only would he be forced to resign his post at the navy department, his dreams for higher public office would have to be abandoned. Louis, working as a mediator between Franklin and Eleanor, made them realize they needed each other in order to succeed.

In July 1920, Franklin resigned as assistant secretary of the navy to run for the office of vice president of the United States with Governor James M. Cox of Ohio. The campaign gave Roosevelt national exposure, and it also gave Eleanor her first political involvement as she traveled with them. Badly defeated by Warren G. Harding in November, Franklin returned to private life. He and Louis Howe began to plan his next campaign as the front-runner candidate for the U.S. Senate. He had every chance for success, yet fate would intervene.

The Onset of Polio

In August 1921, Franklin joined the family at Campobello for their annual vacation. Wednesday night, August 10, he felt the onset of coldlike symptoms, exhaustion, aches, and chills. The following morning, he noticed he had numbness in his left leg,

"We oppose money in politics, we oppose the private control of national finances, we oppose the treatment of human beings as commodities, we oppose starvation wages, we oppose rule by groups or cliques."

and by the next day he was paralyzed from the chest down. Several days later, a specialist was brought in from Boston, who pronounced with certainty Franklin was suffering from infantile paralysis, otherwise known as polio. There was still hope he might recover the use of his legs. Franklin was moved to Presbyterian Hospital in New York and then home on East 36th Street. There the family debated what Franklin's future might be. Sara was adamant he abandon public service and return to Hyde Park to live out the life of a country squire as her husband, James, had done. Eleanor and Louis Howe insisted he should never be treated as an invalid, that his goals were still obtainable.

Keeping his hopes alive for public office fueled his desire to fight for his health. James later wrote, "Struck down by the

The Roosevelt summer home at Campobello, New Brunswick, Canada.

cruelest blow that could have afflicted such an active man, Pa began the struggle not only for his body but for his spirit. No part of it was easy; the proud sprinter experienced the humiliation of learning not just to walk but first to crawl. He battled also against the psychological pressures exerted by an indomitable, worshiping, but misguided, mother, who in her zeal to protect him, tried to sway him toward the easy way out—a hole in the good Roosevelt earth at Hyde Park into which he could crawl and hide, to look out at the world but not to be looked at by it. In this period emerged the FDR of greatness of spirit; he spurned the return to the Hyde Park womb and chose instead to fight his way back."

There had been just one moment of weakness, while still in the throes of the onset of polio, in which Franklin had asked Louis Howe why God had abandoned him. After the diagnosis was made and the facts were clear, Roosevelt never again recognized his own disability, refusing to speak about his feelings on it with anyone. Instead, Franklin threw himself into a lifelong pursuit of recovery. "Straight out of the hospital," Elliott recalled, "Father forced himself into some of the most grueling exercises that a man ever devised for himself, confident that he would make himself walk by sheer effort of will." Franklin would devote the next seven years of his life to the single goal of walking again.

His doctors advised him that swimming was the best possible exercise for his withered muscles, and Franklin headed south to the warm ocean waters off Florida to exercise. In February 1924, he bought a rundown houseboat with Harvard friend John Lawrence, a banker from Boston who had also lost the use of his legs. Christened the *Larooco*—an amalgam of their last names and *co* for company, in a carefully selected lucky double-*o*-and-seven-letters arrangement—Roosevelt cruised the Florida coast, swimming almost daily, fishing, and visiting friends. It was a chance to deal with the loss he had suffered away from family and colleagues. "These were the lonely years," James later wrote. "For a long while during this time of illness and recovery, we had no tangible father, no father-in-being, whom we could touch and talk to at will—only an abstract symbol, a cheery letter writer."

"He has the power to strike at error and wrongdoing that makes his adversaries quail before him. He has a personality that carries to every bearer not only the sincerity but the righteousness of what he says. He is the happy warrior of the political battlefield."

An opportunity to return to the public arena pulled Franklin back to life. In August 1924, he gave the nomination speech for New York Governor Al Smith at the Democratic national convention in the sweltering Madison Square Garden in New York. His sixteen-year-old son James was at his side until the final steps to the rostrum, which Franklin made alone on his crutches before the entire silent crowd of delegates. A fall would have left him helpless on the floor, his career perhaps ruined instantly. "He was thin and pale," wrote Frances Perkins. "He struggled along the platform on crutches, smiling only when he reached the security of the speaker's rostrum. When he smiled at last, his face had a warm friendliness that included everyone in the auditorium. He seemed to be sharing his personal victory . . ." The auditorium roared with cheers for Roosevelt.

FDR gave a rousing speech for Al Smith, declaring: "He has the power to strike at error and wrongdoing that makes his adversaries quail before him. He has a personality that carries to every bearer not only the sincerity but the righteousness of what he says. He is the happy warrior of the political battlefield." The crowd responded with thunderous applause. "I never in my life was as proud of father as I was at that moment," wrote James. "It heightened his image as nothing had ever done. The phrase 'the happy warrior' was used to describe the candidate, but it better described father than the nominee. That hour or so stolen from his sickness made more of father than it did of the man he nominated."

Franklin turned down any talk of his seeking political office. He knew he was still too weak for campaigning, and he was determined to rid himself of crutches. His quest to find a cure led him to Warm Springs, Georgia, that October with Eleanor and secretary "Missy" LeHand at his side. An old friend George Foster Peabody had told him about the

FDR swimming at the pool in Warm Springs, 1930.

"He learned how to laugh again in Warm Springs in the company of others who suffered as he did. Here, he never felt alone or left out."

—James Roosevelt.

legendary waters known for their healing properties. In ancient days, the springs had been sacred ground to the Native Americans where they came to seek cures. In more recent times, it had been a flourishing vacation center when nineteenth-century Georgians flocked there to bathe. The only vestiges of its heyday as a winter resort were a ramshackle hotel, some tumbledown cottages, and a deserted auditorium. As Franklin remembered his first sight of the spa, "Everything was closed, and almost everything was falling to pieces. Most of the roofs leaked . . . It was in awful condition."

Yet the first swim in the hot mineral waters was a turning point in Roosevelt's recovery. Deep from within the earth came an amazing 1,800 gallons a minute of water heated to a constant eighty-nine degrees Fahrenheit. Enriched with minerals, the waters proved as buoyant as the sea. Franklin discovered he could stand in neck-deep water unassisted and edge into shallower depth placing more weight onto his withered leg muscles. In a few weeks, he wrote to Eleanor, "The legs are really improving a great deal. The walking and general exercising in the water is fine, and I have worked out some special exercises, also. This is really a discovery of a place, and there is no doubt that I've got to do it some more. . . ."

Warm Springs would become much more to FDR than a place of physical recovery. Tucked away in the western foothills of Georgia, Meriwether County was mostly rural farmland that relied on cotton. Since the end of the First World War, cotton

FRANKLIN, ELEANOR, AND FAMILY

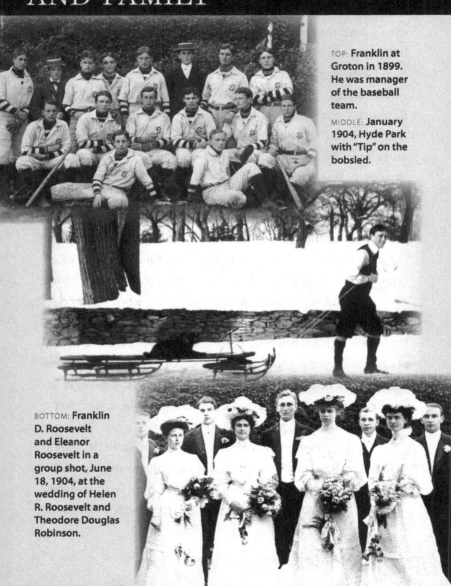

TOP: **Franklin at Groton in 1899. He was manager of the baseball team.**

MIDDLE: **January 1904, Hyde Park with "Tip" on the bobsled.**

BOTTOM: **Franklin D. Roosevelt and Eleanor Roosevelt in a group shot, June 18, 1904, at the wedding of Helen R. Roosevelt and Theodore Douglas Robinson.**

TOP: **Roosevelt family, July 1920.**

MIDDLE: **Franklin at the wheel of *Amberjack II* as he and his party took off for Campobello Island June 16, 1933.**

BOTTOM: **Franklin Roosevelt, 1933.**

prices had fallen by 65 percent and tobacco by 50 percent. As Franklin was driven around the countryside and met the local people, he was struck by the endemic poverty—the shanty homes, the dirt roads, and entire communities without electricity. He met with the people and learned of their troubles, such as the lack of markets for their crops, poor education, and a plague of weevils that destroyed crops. He saw, as he did everywhere he lived, things that could be improved, and he began formulating plans to help by using the power of the federal government to assist. Warm Springs, in short, became a vital education for Franklin. Biographer Frank Friedel noted, "Roosevelt [came] to know and appreciate the thinking of a number of quite ordinary people. . . . The plain people of the South were not an abstraction to Roosevelt; he regarded them as his friends and neighbors."

> "The plain people of the South were not an abstraction to Roosevelt; he regarded them as his friends and neighbors."
> —Frank Friedel

On April 29, 1926, Roosevelt purchased the resort, investing $201,667, which was roughly two-thirds of his entire fortune. He created the nonprofit Georgia Warm Springs Foundation a year later. By the middle of the first full year under

Franklin's overall management, the Warm Springs hydrotherapy facilities were booked to their capacity of sixty-one patients. The progress of the Georgia Warm Springs Foundation and its offspring National Foundation for Infantile Paralysis brought more satisfaction to him in the field of social achievement than anything he accomplished as a government leader, with the possible exception of the Social Security Administration. Although FDR never regained the use of his legs, his experience at Warm Springs helping others was a recovery of the soul. Gone were the endless days of drifting about in the *Larooco*. "He learned how to laugh again in Warm Springs," wrote his son James, "in the company of others who suffered as he did. Here, he never felt alone or left out."

A Return to Politics

By the summer of 1928, Roosevelt had achieved through perseverance and determination a "splendid deception" of appearing to walk with a cane and the assistance of a supporting arm. Crutches, Franklin knew, were political poison. A cane, however, was genteel. Everything possible was done to conceal his disability. The heavy steel braces were painted black and worn under long-cut slacks, and Roosevelt's sons learned to walk with a slow gait to minimize their father's movements to onlookers. Together, they would smile broadly, joke, and wave to the crowd as they moved along slowly. The goal was simply to move from a doorway to a waiting car or to a lectern. They became so adept at it that few people really knew that FDR was crippled; his radiance in public helped mask the disability. Reporter Ernest K. Lindley noted, "The thing about Roosevelt that necessarily strikes you when you see him walking the first time is the thing about him of which you first become unconscious."

His appearance at the Democratic National Convention in Houston in August 1928 would demonstrate his regained vigor. Once again, Franklin would nominate Al Smith for president, this time broadcast by radio to a national audience. A *New York World* reporter described the scene: "Here on the stage is Franklin Roosevelt, a figure tall and proud even in suffering, pale with years of struggle against paralysis, a man softened and cleansed and illumined with pain. For the moment, we are lifted up."

Again, Roosevelt wowed the assembled delegates, this time by appearing to walk to the lectern. "We offer one who has the will to win, who not only deserves success, but commands it. Victory is his habit—the happy warrior, Alfred E. Smith." Once again, the victory was truly Roosevelt's. In the November election, Smith was badly defeated by republican Herbert Hoover, and Franklin was elected as governor of New York— the post Smith had resigned to run for the White House.

Roosevelt was sworn in as governor on the last day of January 1929, with twenty-one-year-old James at his side. It took place in the same room where distant cousin Theodore was

FDR takes over as governor of New York from Al Smith in January 1929. Son James is in the background.

sworn in at the governor's mansion thirty years earlier, using the same Dutch family bible. The stock market crash of October 1929 proved the new governor's mettle as he tackled the crisis. He created the first state-organized program of relief for the unemployed, the Temporary Emergency Relief Administration, which became a forerunner of the federal public works projects he would later enact as president. In 1930, Franklin was reelected by a margin of more than 700,000 votes, placing him as the front-runner for the Democratic presidential nomination in 1932.

Accepting his party's nomination that June in Chicago,

Franklin D. Roosevelt and Eleanor Roosevelt en route to
Washington, D.C., November 8, 1935.

Roosevelt announced: "Throughout the nation, men and women, forgotten in the political philosophy of the government, look to us here for guidance and for more equitable opportunity to share in the distribution of national wealth . . . . I pledge myself to a new deal for the American people. This is more than a political campaign. It is a call to arms." As Franklin explained to a friend, this was a new deck of cards in the poker game of life. The New Deal had been born.

On election night, Roosevelt's victory was so complete, one man wired Herbert Hoover saying, "Vote for Roosevelt and make it unanimous." It had been a victory not only of politics but a triumph of spirit over adversity to conquer physical paralysis. Franklin Delano Roosevelt would take that same drive, energy, and will to the White House, as he took charge during the worst national crisis since the Civil War. For the next twelve years, he would not only lead the country through depression and war but implement a vision of a new world peace by helping to establish the United Nations in 1945. Championing the idea that the federal government has a social duty to help improve the lives of all Americans, he altered the political landscape forever. No American president before or since has accomplished so much. He still defines for many today the role of president and the greatness of the United States of America.

2

On Leadership

Of the many great attributes of Franklin Roosevelt's political skills, perhaps the best was his sense of timing. He knew exactly when to invoke the prestige of his office for maximum effect. He took this far beyond campaigning and politics. Franklin knew he was the most visible and powerful symbol of hope for millions of people affected by disability, yet keeping the public unaware of his crippled condition was the goal of his "splendid deception." He was helped by a press corps that was especially close to him, with whom there was a gentleman's agreement that no photos would be published portraying him in a wheelchair or otherwise disadvantaged.

It is interesting to note the rare occasions when FDR allowed himself to be seen publicly in a wheelchair. He was always comfortable at Warm Springs where he visited not only with other patients but with wounded veterans. In July 1944,

Franklin D. Roosevelt, Fala, and Ruthie Bie
at Hill Top Cottage in Hyde Park, N.Y. , 1941

he sailed to Pearl Harbor to confer with General Douglas Mac-Arthur and Admiral Chester Nimitz. Afterwards, he went to the amputee ward of a military hospital in his wheelchair. He went by each bed, allowing the men to see him exactly as he was. He became a hero in the eyes of many as he advocated on behalf of others with disabilities.

Marine General Evans Carlson witnessed one such occasion in the fall of 1935. While in Georgia for Thanksgiving, the president arrived at Warm Springs to attend a Sunday evening devotional. Carlson later described the scene in a letter to Missy LeHand: "We had placed a chair at the roadside for the president's use, but when he drove up, he waved the chair aside. Descending from the car, he drew himself up, and with magnificent dignity and superb will, he walked down the ramp through the door and forward to his seat amid the patients. Never will I forget that walk, which was performed in utter silence. No explanation was ever given for what must have been a supreme effort. But I sensed, and I felt others present must have sensed, that it was made for the purpose of giving hope and inspiration to the assembled patients."

> We must be the great arsenal of Democracy.
>
> —Fireside Chat, December 29, 1940.

Let me assert my firm belief that the only thing we have to fear is fear itself— nameless, unreasoning, unjustified terror which paralyzes needed efforts to convert retreat into advance.

—First Inaugural Address, March 4, 1933.

I never forget that I live in a house owned by all the American people and that I have been given their trust. . . . I want to be sure that neither battles nor burdens of office shall ever blind me to an intimate knowledge of the way the American people want to live and the simple purposes they put me here for.

—Fireside Chat, April 14, 1938

FDR in Harrisburg, Virginia, 1936

Government can err; Presidents do make mistakes, but the immortal Dante tells us that divine justice weighs the sins of the cold-blooded and the sins of the warm-hearted in different scales. Better the occasional faults of a government that lives in a spirit of charity than the consistent omissions of a government frozen in the ice of its own indifference.

—Acceptance speech for the renomination for the Presidency, June 27, 1936

In regard to every problem that arises, there are counselors these days who say: "Do nothing"; other counselors who say: "Do everything." Common sense dictates an avoidance of both extremes. I say to you: "Do something"; and when you have done that something, if it works, do it some more; and if it does not work, then do something else.

—Address to the Young Democratic Club, Baltimore, Maryland,
April 13, 1936

Let us not be afraid to help each other—let us never forget that government is ourselves and not an alien power over us. The ultimate rulers of our democracy are not a President and Senators and Congressmen and government officials but the voters of this country.

—Address at Marietta, Ohio, July 8, 1938

I pledge you, I pledge myself, to a new deal for the American people.

—Acceptance speech for the Democratic Party nomination for President, 1932

If I read the temper of our people correctly, we now realize as we have never realized before our interdependence on each other; that we cannot merely take but we must give as well; that if we are to go forward, we must move as a trained and loyal army willing to sacrifice for the good of a common discipline, because without such discipline no progress is made, no leadership becomes effective.

—First Inaugural Address, March 4, 1933

The country needs and, unless I mistake its temper, the country demands bold, persistent experimentation. It is common sense to take a method and try it: If it fails, admit it frankly and try another. But above all, try something.

—Address at Oglethorpe University, May 22, 1932

Government is competent when all who compose it work as trustees for the whole people. It can make constant progress when it keeps abreast of all the facts. It can obtain justified support and legitimate criticism when the people receive true information of all that government does.

—Second Inaugural Address, January 20, 1937

I have no expectation of making a hit every time I come to bat. What I seek is the highest possible batting average, not only for myself but for the team. Theodore Roosevelt once said to me: "If I can be right 75 percent of the time, I shall come up to the fullest measure of my hopes."

—Fireside Chat, May 7, 1933

I should like to have it said of my first Administration that in it the forces of selfishness and of lust for power met their match. I should like to have it said of my second Administration that in it these forces met their master.

—Speech at Madison Square Garden, October 31, 1936

Franklin D. Roosevelt aboard
the USS *Indianapolis*, 1936.

No man can occupy the office of
President without realizing that he is
President of all the people.

—Speech at Madison Square Garden, October 31, 1936

A man comes to wisdom in many years of public life. He knows well that when the light of favor shines upon him, it comes not, of necessity, that he himself is important. Favor comes because for a brief moment in the great space of human change and progress, some general human purpose finds in him a satisfactory embodiment.

—Remarks at Poughkeepsie, New York, November 8, 1932

We shall strive for perfection. We shall not achieve it immediately — but we shall strive. We may make mistakes, but they must never be mistakes which result from faintness of heart or abandonment of moral principle.

—Fourth Inaugural Address, January 20, 1945

A migrant mother of seven children, photographed by Dorothy Lange of the Farm Security Administration at Nipomo, California, in 1936.

On Poverty

O*ne of the most remarkable times in Franklin Roosevelt's* life occurred during his first years living in Warm Springs, Georgia, before his election as governor of New York. Without the burdens of public office or security concerns, he was free to move about as he pleased. Franklin's mobility and freedom were greatly enhanced by obtaining a car with hand-operated controls, enabling him to drive around. He loved driving, stopping at any opportunity to say hello to the local farmers and townspeople of Warm Springs. He became "almost as familiar to the agrarian population as the rural mail carrier," one local resident remarked. "There was a difference; the mail carrier did take Sundays off."

Living in Georgia became a political education for Franklin as he saw firsthand the poor economic conditions of the region. It gave him valuable experience talking to ordinary people and explaining complex issues. Biographer Frank Friedel noted, "Roosevelt came to know and appreciate the thinking of a number of quite ordinary people. . . . The plain people of the South were not an abstraction to Roosevelt; he regarded them as his friends and neighbors."

Franklin saw the forces of modern industrial society advance the nation yet also create new problems for average Americans. Speaking in 1936, he declared: "Out of this modern civilization, economic royalists carved new dynasties. New kingdoms were built upon concentration of control over material things. Through new uses of corporations, banks, and securities, new machinery of industry and agriculture, of labor and capital . . . the whole structure of modern life was impressed into this royal service." The result was a vast loss

Franklin D. Roosevelt sitting in his Model T meets with two young friends in Warm Springs, Georgia, November 1931.

of freedom for most Americans as, Roosevelt continued, "the hours men and women worked, the wages they received, the conditions of their labor—these had passed beyond the control of the people and were imposed by this new industrial dictatorship . . . . Private enterprise, indeed, became too private. It became privileged enterprise, not free enterprise."

The poor economic conditions in and around Warm Springs were evidence of those effects. Farmers could not find markets for their crops, even as trainloads of goods from other states passed through to the booming cities of Florida. Entire communities were without electrical power, adequate food, or shelter. As familiar as he had become with urban poverty, after witnessing the slums of New York as a student, he now saw the effects of sustained, endemic rural poverty. It was in the backwoods of Georgia that Roosevelt began formulating some of the plans that would become hallmarks of his presidency: the Tennessee Valley Authority, the Social Security Act, and the Agricultural Adjustment Administration, among others. He saw the power of the federal government was needed to step in and offer assistance to the states, which could not afford improvements on a vast scale. FDR's experience with poverty became a critical stepping-stone to the presidency.

> "And now abideth faith, hope, and charity, these three; but the greatest of these is charity."
>
> —I Corinthians XIII, v. 13

The lessons of history, confirmed by the evidence immediately before me, show conclusively that continued dependence upon relief induces a spiritual and moral disintegration fundamentally destructive to the national fiber. To dole out relief in this way is to administer a narcotic, a subtle destroyer of the human spirit. It is inimical to the dictates of sound policy. It is in violation of the traditions of America. Work must be found for able-bodied but destitute workers.

—Second State of the Union Address, January 4, 1935

*We are determined to make every American citizen
the subject of his country's interest and concern; and
we will never regard any faithful law-abiding group
within our borders as superfluous. The test of our
progress is not whether we add more to the abundance
of those who have much; it is whether we provide
enough for those who have too little.*

—Second Inaugural Address, January 20, 1937

*No country, however rich, can afford the waste of its
human resources. Demoralization caused by vast
unemployment is our greatest extravagance. Morally,
it is the greatest menace to our social order.*

—Fireside Chat, September 30, 1934

One of the greatest lessons that the city dwellers have come to understand in these past two years is this: Empty pocketbooks on the farm do not turn factory wheels in the city.

—Address on the Agricultural Adjustment Act, May 14, 1935

We are poor indeed if this nation cannot afford to lift from every recess of American life the dread fear of the unemployed that they are not needed in the world. We cannot afford to accumulate a deficit in the books of human fortitude. In the place of the palace of privilege, we seek to build a temple out of faith and hope and charity.

—Address at the Democratic National Convention, June 27, 1936

Prosperity measured in dollars is coming back. There is none among you to deny it. But there is a higher measure for prosperity: the measure of permanency, the measure of security. We seek not the prosperity of 1929 but the kind which will mean to every American family an assurance of safety of the home, safety of old age, safety of savings, safety of employment.

—Address at Providence, Rhode Island, October 21, 1936

4

On America

The United States was a sacred place for Franklin Roosevelt. At the center of his love for country was the Roosevelt family's Springwood estate at Hyde Park. The home is now a national historic site and presidential library, and anyone visiting it today will understand its special place in Franklin's life. Set upon a high bank of the Hudson River, it commands a majestic view of the river valley, the forested landscape stretching as far as the eye can see. With its quiet fields and vast stretches of trees, many planted by Franklin personally, it is a gentle and peaceful place that must have been a perfect little heaven for a small boy growing to love the nature that abounded outside. As president, he had returned to his home on two hundred occasions, making it, in effect, an alternate White House. It makes perfect sense, however, that he would return home to look out from peace and perfection to contemplate the issues of an imperfect world.

Franklin well understood the country had vastly changed in the century since his home was first constructed. The

Springwood estate in fall.

Franklin campaigning in 1920.

United States was evolving in his lifetime into a mechanized society pushed forever forward by technology, mass production, and a growing urbanization. The vast frontiers of America, where enterprising souls could once journey and make themselves over, had disappeared. He saw instead "a frontier of the spirit," which called upon Americans to seek improvements in their lives with the resources and talents at hand. He saw the role of the federal government as a key element, providing security for Americans as they made their way in the new industrialized society and replacing the old protections of kinships and small communities. In his view, America would achieve a new prosperity. "All over this nation, we are hewing out a commonwealth—a commonwealth of the states, which we hope will give to its people more truly than any that has gone before, the fulfillment of

"Out of the Cox campaign, he brought a firm conviction that agricultural and industrial life could be made much better for the people by conscious government programs."

—Frances Perkins

security, of freedom, of opportunity, and of happiness, which America asks and which America is entitled to receive."

There were lessons Franklin had learned while traveling around the country. When he campaigned for vice president with James Cox in 1920, he saw other regions and acquired valuable political insights. "He found that the interests of the people were in their jobs, families, security, and future rather than in political theories," noted Frances Perkins. "Party platforms left them cold and puzzled. He learned a great deal about America, too. As a farmer from a well-watered valley in New York, he learned that irrigation rights are life-and-death matters in the West and Southwest. He was a keen observer, asked hundreds of questions, and increased his knowledge of the land he was to serve one day as president. Out of the Cox campaign, he brought a firm conviction that agricultural and industrial life could be made much better for the people by conscious government programs."

This was the heart of the New Deal, to establish protections for the freedoms and rights of people so they might prosper in a society dominated by industry. The New Deal represented the best of what Americans were made of—ingenuity, compromise, and cooperation. It seemed natural to Franklin that Americans would roll up their sleeves and take on the tasks of this new frontier as eagerly and with the same fortitude with which they once confronted the immense challenges of moving west.

> Among American citizens, there should be no forgotten men and no forgotten races.
> —Address at Howard University, Washington, D.C., October 26, 1936

When Andrew Jackson, "Old Hickory," died, someone asked, "Will he go to heaven?" and the answer was, "He will if he wants to." If I am asked whether the American people will pull themselves out of this Depression, I answer, "They will if they want to."

—Fireside Chat, July 24, 1933

FDR's third inauguration, January 1941.

In the face of great perils never before encountered, our strong purpose is to protect and to perpetuate the integrity of democracy. For this, we muster the spirit of America and the faith of America. We do not retreat. We are not content to stand still. As Americans, we go forward, in the service of our country, by the will of God.

—Third Inaugural Address, January 20, 1941

The saving grace of America lies in the fact that the overwhelming majority of Americans are possessed of two great qualities: a sense of humor and a sense of proportion.

—Address at Savannah, Georgia, November 18, 1933

There is a mysterious cycle in human events. To some generations, much is given. Of other generations, much is expected. This generation of Americans has a rendezvous with destiny.

—Democratic National Convention, June 27, 1936

America is not a country which can be confounded by the appeasers, the defeatists, the backstairs manufacturers of panic. It is a country that talks out its problems in the open, where any man can hear them.

—Speech at the White House Correspondents' Association Dinner, March 15, 1941

We Americans are not destroyers— we are builders.

—Fireside Chat, December 9, 1941

The United States does not consider it a sacrifice to do all one can, to give one's best to our nation, when the nation is fighting for its existence and its future life.

—Fireside Chat, December 9, 1941

Disorder is not an American habit. Self-help and self-control are the essence of the American tradition.

—Annual Message to Congress, January 3, 1934

The vigor of our history comes largely from the fact that as a comparatively young nation, we have gone fearlessly ahead doing things that were never done before.

—Address to the Young Democratic Club, Baltimore, Maryland, April 13, 1936

Young boys employed as day laborers at a cranberry bog, 1938.

5

On Labor

On Saturday, March 25, 1911, a devastating industrial accident occurred in New York City. At 4:40 pm, a fire broke out on the eighth floor of the Asch Building, a ten-story brick structure on the corner of Greene Street and Washington Place in lower Manhattan. The Triangle Shirtwaist Company occupied the top three floors of the building. Most of the workers on the eighth and tenth floors were able to evacuate, but word failed to reach the ninth floor quickly. Fire enveloped one of the two stairwells, while the doors to the other had been locked shut by the owners, trapping some two hundred people in the inferno. Of the 148 people who lost their lives that day, sixty-two had chosen to jump, as a horrified crowd watched from below. One of those onlookers was a young woman named Frances Perkins.

The Triangle Shirtwaist fire inspired Perkins in her crusade for social reform, serving as the first female member of the New York State Industrial Commission at the invitation of Governor Al Smith. In 1929, Franklin Roosevelt, following Smith to the governor's mansion, offered her the job of state industrial commissioner. She tirelessly led a campaign for better working conditions, protection for women, laws against child labor, shorter working hours, and unemployment insurance. By FDR's election as president in 1933, she had become a cornerstone of the New Deal and served as secretary of labor for the next twelve years. In essence, she became what some have termed Roosevelt's social conscience.

During his seven years as assistant secretary of the navy, FDR gained experience meeting with labor unions and hearing the concerns of working men. As he traveled the country with James Cox as vice presidential candidate in 1920, it broadened his thinking to other regions of the country where people faced different challenges. When he went to Warm Springs for the first time seeking a cure for his paralysis, he witnessed rural poverty—the one-room schoolhouses, shanty homes with dirt floors, entire communities without electricity, and the devastation to farms due to the loss of viable markets. It was in the backwoods of Georgia that FDR began formulating plans for economic recovery.

Frances Perkins, secretary of labor.

An unemployed worker, New York City docks.

By the time Roosevelt accepted the nomination of the Democratic Party to run for the presidency against Herbert Hoover on July 2, 1932, the "forgotten man" was foremost on his mind as a centerpiece for the campaign. "Throughout the nation, men and women, forgotten in the political philosophy of the government of the last years, look to us here for guidance and for more equitable opportunity to share in the distribution of national wealth. On the farms, in the large metropolitan areas, in the smaller cities, and in the villages, millions of our citizens cherish the hope that their old standards of living and of thought have not gone forever. Those millions cannot and shall not hope in vain."

I see an America where factory workers are not discarded after they reach their prime, where there is no endless chain of poverty from generation to generation, where impoverished farmers and farm hands do not become homeless wanderers, where monopoly does not make youth a beggar for a job.

—Campaign Address at Cleveland, Ohio, November 2, 1940

No business which depends for existence on paying less than living wages to its workers has any right to continue in this country.

—Statement on the National Industrial Recovery Act, June 16, 1933

The object of government is the welfare of the people. The liberty of the people to carry on their business should not be abridged unless the larger interests of the many are concerned.

When the interests of the many are concerned, the interests of the few must yield. It is the purpose of the government to see not only that the legitimate interests of the few are protected but that the welfare and the rights of the many are conserved. These are the principles which we must remember in any consideration of the question.

This, I take it, is sound government—not politics. Those are the essential basic conditions under which government can be of service.

—Campaign Address, Portland, Oregon, September 21, 1932

It is to the real advantage of every producer, every manufacturer, and every merchant to cooperate in the improvement of working conditions, because the best customer of American industry is the well-paid worker.

—Address at Cleveland, Ohio, October 16, 1936

In the Cotton Textile Code and in other agreements already signed, child labor has been abolished. That makes me personally happier than any other one thing with which I have been connected since I came to Washington.

—Fireside Chat. July 24, 1933

It is one of the characteristics of a free and democratic nation that it has free and independent labor unions.

—Speech to Teamsters Union, September 11, 1940

The Unemployed Union in the city of Camden, New Jersey, marches south on Broadway in New York City.

On Politics

Franklin Roosevelt was a master politician. It was said he could lay out a map of the United States, draw a line from the Atlantic to the Pacific, and be able to name every county along that line and the names of every Democratic Party chairman in each one. Roosevelt was known for his consummate political skill—his ability to deal with government bureaucracy, to navigate party politics and special interests, and still address the needs of the people. He also knew the importance of consensus building in Washington, appointing key Republicans to his cabinet.

Above all, Roosevelt possessed a magnificent sense of timing. He understood when to invoke the prestige of the presidency and when to hold it in reserve. Combining all his talents with a vision for the country's future, his personal charisma and eloquence speaking to the American people, he accomplished more in the realm of politics than any president before or since. New York Governor Al Smith said of Roosevelt, "He was the kindest man you ever met, but just don't get in his way."

Franklin making a radio broadcast in 1934.

We oppose money in politics, we oppose the private control of national finances, we oppose the treatment of human beings as commodities, we oppose starvation wages, we oppose rule by groups or cliques.

—Accepting the vice presidential nomination, August 9, 1920

Our party must be a party of liberal thought, of planned action, of enlightened international outlook, and of the greatest good to the greatest number of our citizens.

—Presidential nomination address, July 2, 1932

Franklin D. Roosevelt with Louis Howe, Tom Lynch, and Marvin MacIntyre, 1920.

Our Republican leaders tell us economic laws—sacred, inviolable, unchangeable— cause panics which no one could prevent. But while they prate of economic laws, men and women are starving. We must lay hold of the fact that economic laws are not made by nature. They are made by human beings.

—Address at the Democratic National Convention, July 2, 1932

Never before in modern history have the essential differences between the two major American parties stood out in such striking contrast as they do today. Republican leaders not only have failed in material things, they have failed in national vision, because in disaster they have held out no hope, they have pointed out no path for the people below to climb back to places of security and of safety in our American life.

—Presidential nomination address, Chicago, Illinois, July 2, 1932

Now, there is an old and somewhat lugubrious adage which says: "Never speak of rope in the house of a man who has been hanged." In the same way, if I were a Republican leader speaking to a mixed audience, the last word in the whole dictionary that I think I would use is that word **depression***.*

—Campaign Dinner Address, Washington, DC, September 23, 1944

The highest duty of any government is to order public affairs so that opportunities for youth shall be made ever broader and firmer . . . The school is the last expenditure upon which America should be willing to economize.

—Campaign Address at Kansas City, Missouri, October 13, 1936

The true conservative is the man who has a real concern for injustices and takes thought against the day of reckoning.

—Speech in Syracuse, New York, September 29, 1936

Make it simple enough for the women to understand and then the men will understand.

—advice on campaign literature to Frances Perkins, 1936

You can't be a great president without being a great politician. . . . You make as few and as small compromises as you must to make your way to the top. You don't want to be compromised by your compromises.

—comment to James Roosevelt

A radical is a man with both feet firmly planted—in the air. A conservative is a man with two perfectly good legs who, however, has never learned to walk forward. A reactionary is a somnambulist walking backwards. A liberal is a man who uses his legs and his hands at the behest—at the command—of his head.

—Radio Address to the *New York Herald Tribune* Forum, October 26, 1939

Sometimes you have to deny your political opposition the paint they need to present the public the picture of you they want to show. You can't feed your enemies ammunition.

—comment to James Roosevelt prior to re-election for a third term in 1940

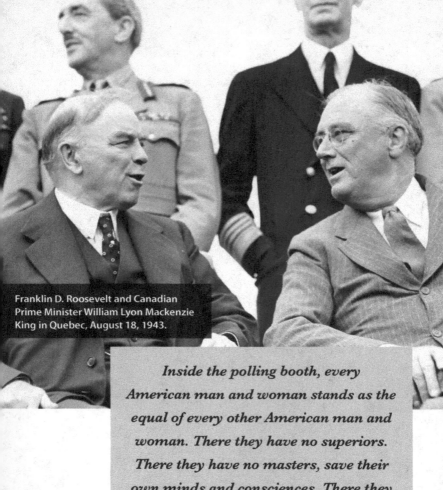

Franklin D. Roosevelt and Canadian Prime Minister William Lyon Mackenzie King in Quebec, August 18, 1943.

Inside the polling booth, every American man and woman stands as the equal of every other American man and woman. There they have no superiors. There they have no masters, save their own minds and consciences. There they are sovereign American citizens.

—Address at Worcester, Massachusetts, October 21, 1936

The future lies with those wise
political leaders who realize that the
great public is interested more in
government than politics.

—Jackson Day Dinner Address, Washington, D.C., January 8, 1940

❧

A government can be no better
than the public opinion that
sustains them.

—Jackson Day Dinner Address, Washington, D.C., January 8, 1936

On Freedom

To many observers in 1933, democracy in America and around the world appeared to be dying. Violent revolution lay just beneath the smoldering mood of desperation that prevailed in the United States. As Franklin Roosevelt took office, banks were closing around the country, production was nearly at a standstill, and in the Midwest, farmers rallied to block the foreclosure of their lands. Throughout the country, fourteen million people were out of work. Tens of thousands of families were losing their homes, and nine million people had lost their life savings. People were down and out in their feelings, not only in their stomachs and in their pocketbooks. Eli Ginzberg, a member of the president's administration, remembered, "It was a tremendously depressing period of time. There were not a few people who really saw the possibility that the country was going to disintegrate."

Franklin saw the true nature of the struggle as everyday people tried to make a living under the worst effects of the Depression. "Necessitous men are not free men," he noted in a 1936 address. "Liberty requires opportunity to make a living—a living decent according to the standard of the time, a living which gives man not only enough to live by, but something to live for."

The New Deal was far more than an economic recovery. It was a restoration in the confidence and spirit of free government. As the rise of fascist governments in other lands rose to challenge this concept, Franklin spoke plainly on what was at stake. "In this world of ours in other lands, there are some people, who, in times past, have lived and fought for freedom, and seem to have grown too weary to carry on the fight. They have sold their heritage of freedom for the illusion of a living. They have yielded their democracy."

Thus, Franklin linked economic progress and security in America to the defense of democracies abroad. In November 1940, as England stood alone against the Nazi onslaught and American diplomacy with Japan was failing, the president assured Americans of the ultimate triumph. "All we have known of the glories of democracy—its freedom, its efficiency as a mode of living, its ability to meet the aspirations of the common man—all these are merely an introduction to the greater story of a more glorious future."

"The New Deal" alfresco by Conrad A. Albrizio, dedicated to President Roosevelt, is in the auditorium of the Leonardo Da Vinci Art School.

If the fires of freedom and civil liberties burn low in other lands, they must be made brighter in our own. If in other lands the press and books and literature of all kinds are censored, we must redouble our efforts here to keep them free. If in other lands the eternal truths of the past are threatened by intolerance, we must provide a safe place for their perception.

—Address before the National Education Association. New York City, June 30, 1938

We intend to keep our freedom—to defend it from attacks from without and against corruption from within. We shall defend it against the forces of dictatorship, whatever disguises and false faces they may wear. But we have learned that freedom in itself is not enough. Freedom of speech is of no use to a man who has nothing to say. Freedom of worship is of no use to a man who has lost his God. Democracy, to be dynamic, must provide for its citizens opportunity as well as freedom.

—Campaign Address at Cleveland, Ohio, November 2, 1940

I still believe in ideals. I am not for a return to that definition of Liberty under which for many years a free people were being gradually regimented into the service of the privileged few. I prefer and I am sure you prefer that broader definition of Liberty under which we are moving forward to greater freedom, to greater security for the average man than he has ever known before in the history of America.

—Fireside Chat, September 30, 1934

Those who cherish their freedom and recognize and respect the equal right of their neighbors to be free and live in peace must work together for the triumph of law and moral principles in order that peace, justice, and confidence may prevail in the world. There must be a return to a belief in the pledged word, in the value of a signed treaty. There must be recognition of the fact that national morality is as vital as private morality.

—Quarantine Speech, Chicago, Illinois, October 5, 1937

I produce ... I sell ... I buy ...

VICTORY FOOD SPECIALS

ASK YOUR GROCER

True individual freedom cannot exist without economic security and independence. People who are hungry and out of a job are the stuff of which dictatorships are made. In the truest sense, freedom cannot be bestowed; it must be achieved.

—On the anniversary of the Emancipation Proclamation, September 16, 1936

*Human kindness has never weakened the stamina
or softened the fiber of a free people.
A nation does not have to be cruel in order to be
tough. The vigorous expression of our American
community spirit is truly important.*

—Radio Address for the Mobilization for Human Needs,
October 13, 1940

A world turned into a stereotype, a society converted into a regiment, a life translated into a routine, make it difficult for either art or artists to survive. Crush individuality in society, and you crush art as well. Nourish the conditions for a free life, and you nourish the arts, too.

—Radio Dedication of the Museum of Modern Art, May 10, 1939

It is a good thing to demand liberty for ourselves and for those who agree with us, but it is a better thing and rarer thing to give liberty to others who do not agree with us.

—Radio Address on Maryland Tercentenary Celebration, November 22, 1933

Democracy is the practice of self-government and is a covenant among free men to respect the rights and liberties of their fellow man.

—Annual Message to Congress, Washington, D.C., January 4, 1939

This nation has placed its destiny in the hands and heads and hearts of its millions of free men and women; and its faith in freedom under the guidance of God. Freedom means the supremacy of human rights everywhere. Our support goes to those who struggle to gain those rights or keep them. Our strength is our unity of purpose. To that high concept there can be no end save victory.

—State of the Union "Four Freedoms" Speech, January 6, 1941

8

On War and Peace

On January 30, 1933, a month before Franklin Roosevelt was sworn in as 32nd President of the United States, Adolf Hitler took the oath of office as Chancellor of Germany. For the next twelve years, the fate of the world was largely decided by this one man, who aimed above all to reverse the German losses of the First World War and create a new German empire based on racial purity and military might. By 1939, the German military had secretly rearmed, reclaimed the Rhineland, effected unification with Austria, and then demanded the Sudetenland, then part of Czechoslovakia. A new European war appeared imminent.

FDR played no decisive role in these events. Disillusioned by the wartime experiences of the First World War, the United States Senate had refused to join the League of Nations in 1919, returning the country to a state of passive neutrality.

U.S.S. *Arizona* burning, morning of December 7, 1941.

Americans wanted no part in any future European conflicts. To crown the mood of isolationism, Congress enacted the Neutrality Act of 1935, banning the sale of arms and material to warring nations and slashing military spending. By September 1939, the United States Army ranked eighteenth in the world's armies and had few modern weapons.

Yet FDR realized the nature and threat of war had changed. As technology had revolutionized industry, so too had it altered the conduct of warfare. More alarming still was the political and economic threat posed by the formal alliance between Germany, Italy, and Japan, created by the Tripartite Pact in September 1940. Combined, these powerful forces threatened to cut off England and the United States from the rest of the world. In September 1939, when England and France declared war on Germany over the invasion of Poland, both nations looked to the United States for help. It would take all of FDR's political mastery to overcome his nation's neutrality laws to provide aid.

> "War is a contagion, whether it be declared or undeclared."
>
> —FDR "Quarantine Speech," Chicago, October 5, 1937

Not until the defeat of France in June of 1940 did American public opinion, stunned by the dynamic German attack against Western Europe, begin to shift in FDR's direction. President Roosevelt immediately bypassed the Neutrality Acts by declaring many millions of rounds of American ammunition

Divine Service at the Atlantic Conference on board the HMS *Prince of Wales*, August 10, 1941.

and guns as surplus and authorizing their shipment to the United Kingdom. On September 2, 1940, Roosevelt authorized the transfer of fifty older destroyers from the United States Navy. It signified that FDR had committed the United States, in spirit if not yet war, to the support of Great Britain.

Roosevelt reasoned that an incident at sea between the American and German navies would precipitate a public outcry that would enable him to ask Congress for a declaration of war. Yet it was from the Japanese that the first blows of war fell, at Pearl Harbor on December 7, 1941. On December 8, 1941, the U.S. declared war on Japan and entered the conflict that came to be known as World War II. Once again, Franklin Roosevelt was called upon to lead his nation through one of the darkest chapters in modern history.

I have seen war. I have seen war on land and sea. I have seen blood running from the wounded. I have seen men coughing out their gassed lungs. I have seen the dead in the mud. I have seen cities destroyed. I have seen two hundred limping exhausted men come out of line—the survivors of a regiment of one thousand that went forward forty-eight hours before. I have seen children starving. I have seen the agony of mothers and wives. I hate war.

—Speech at Chautauqua, New York, August 14, 1936

Allied conference in Quebec, on August 18, 1943. Seated are Canadian Prime Minister Mackenzie King, Franklin Roosevelt, and Winston Churchill.

Unless the peace that follows recognizes that the whole world is one neighborhood and does justice to the whole human race, the germs of another world war will remain as a constant threat to mankind.

—Address to White House Correspondents' Association, February 12, 1943.

I wish I could keep war from all nations; but that is beyond my power. I can at least make certain that no act of the United States helps to produce or to promote war. I can at least make clear that the conscience of America revolts against war and that any nation which provokes war forfeits the sympathy of the people of the United States.

—Speech at Chautauqua, New York, August 14, 1936

A dark old world was devastated by wars between conflicting religions.
A dark modern world faces wars between conflicting economic and political fanaticisms in which are intertwined race hatreds.

—Speech at Chautauqua, New York August 14, 1936

There are some timid ones among us who say that we must preserve peace at any price- lest we lose our liberties forever. To them I say this: never in the history of the world has a nation lost its democracy by a successful struggle to defend its democracy. We must not be defeated by the fear of the very danger which we are preparing to resist. Our freedom has shown its ability to survive war, but our freedom would never survive surrender.

—Fireside Chat, May 27, 1941

We can gain no lasting peace if we approach it with suspicion and mistrust or with fear. We can gain it only if we proceed with the understanding, the confidence, and the courage which flow from conviction. The Almighty God has blessed our land in many ways. He has given our people stout hearts and strong arms with which to strike mighty blows for freedom and truth. He has given to our country a faith which has become the hope of all peoples in an anguished world. So we pray to Him now for the vision to see our way clearly to see the way that leads to a better life for ourselves and for all our fellow men—and to the achievement of His will to peace on earth.

—Fourth Inaugural Address, January 20, 1945

Franklin D. Roosevelt and Churchill in Casablanca, January 22, 1943.

You must master at the outset a simple but unalterable fact in modern foreign relations. When peace has been broken anywhere, peace of all countries everywhere is in danger.

—Fireside Chat, September 3, 1939

In the days and in the years that are to come, we shall work for a just and honorable peace, a durable peace, as today we work and fight for total victory in war.

—Fourth Inaugural Address, January 20, 1945

There is a solidarity and interdependence about the modern world, both technically and morally, which makes it impossible for any nation completely to isolate itself from economic and political upheavals in the rest of the world, especially when such upheavals appear to be spreading and not declining. There can be no stability or peace either within nations or between nations except under laws and moral standards adhered to by all.

—Quarantine Speech, Chicago, Illinois, October 5, 1937

We seek peace, not only for our generation but also for the generation of our children. I want our great democracy to be wise enough to realize that aloofness from war is not promoted by unawareness of war. In a world of mutual suspicions, peace must be affirmatively reached for. It cannot just be wished for. And it cannot just be waited for.

—Fireside Chat, October 12, 1937

This nation will remain a neutral nation, but I cannot ask that every American remain neutral in thought as well. Even a neutral has a right to take account of facts. Even a neutral cannot be asked to close his mind or close his conscience.

—Fireside Chat, September 3, 1939

No man can tame a tiger into a kitten by stroking it. There can be no appeasement with ruthlessness. There can be no reasoning with an incendiary bomb.

—Fireside Chat, December 29, 1940

We must be the great arsenal of democracy.
For us this is an emergency as serious as war itself.
We must apply ourselves to our task with the same
resolution, the same sense of urgency, the same
spirit of patriotism and sacrifice as we would
show, were we at war.

—Fireside Chat, December 29, 1940

The structure of world peace cannot be the work of one man, or one party, or one nation. It cannot be just an American peace, or a British peace, or a Russian, a French, or a Chinese peace. It cannot be a peace of large nations—or of small nations. It must be a peace which rests on the cooperative effort of the whole world.

—Address before Congress on the Yalta Conference, Washington, D.C.,
March 1, 1945.

It cannot be a structure of complete perfection at first. But it can be a peace—— and it will be a peace—— based on the sound and just principles of the Atlantic Charter—— on the concept of the dignity of the human being—— and on the guarantees of tolerance and freedom of religious worship.

—Address to Congress on Yalta, March 1, 1945

Today we are faced with the preeminent fact that if civilization is to survive the science of human relationship—it must demand the ability of all peoples, of all kinds, to live together in the same world in peace.

—Undelivered address prepared for Jefferson Day to be delivered April 13, 1945

FDR, Tom Lynch, and Louis Howe, 1920.

9

On Friendship

Franklin Roosevelt's affable and good natured public persona hid the deep complexities of the man. His Secretary of Labor, Frances Perkins, called him "the most complex person I ever knew." He was a leader who did not hesitate to ask for opinions, seek advice, and weigh arguments between members of his inner circle. When it came time to make the tough decisions, however, FDR kept the cards close to his chest, and few knew what he was thinking. It is not surprising, then, that he had few intimate friends who knew his mind and stood up to him when they thought he was wrong. Of the many who came to know FDR, two were his most loyal companions—Louis McHenry Howe, his political advisor, and Marguerite "Missy" LeHand, his personal secretary.

Louis Howe, a native of Saratoga Springs, was a local newspaper reporter working the Albany senatorial battle against

Tammany Hall in 1911. Roosevelt had just been elected in an upset campaign from Duchess County and was leading a rebellion against the leadership of his own party to block the nomination of Tammany Hall's candidate for U.S. senate. Impressed by the young man's charisma, Howe quickly became a member of Franklin's staff.

The two made a strange yet dynamic team—the tall, charismatic, Harvard-educated Franklin with money and connections and the short, scar-faced, high-school-educated Louis with experience, political knowledge, and uncanny instincts. As Curtis Roosevelt later said of Howe, "He knew where all the bodies were buried, and F.D.R. needed to know."

It was Howe who single-handedly helped Franklin win a

Franklin appears with the seniors of the Harvard Crimson Board in 1904.

second term in the New York Senate as Roosevelt took months to recover from a serious bout of scarlet fever, and Roosevelt remained loyal to him. Together they proved unbeatable. Howe dedicated himself to promoting Franklin's career to the point that the *New York Times* later referred to him as "The President's Other *I*."

Missy LeHand was from a second-generation Irish family originally from Potsdam, New York, who later moved to Somerville, Massachusetts, where she attended high school. In 1920, Missy was working as a secretary in Washington, D.C., and was hired by FDR's office manager to work at the Democratic campaign's Washington office during Roosevelt's run for the vice presidency. Missy quickly became devoted to Franklin. Impressed by her work ethic and organizational skills, she was asked by the Roosevelt family to become Franklin's personal secretary following the election.

For the next twenty years, Missy was an inseparable companion to Franklin. When polio struck him down in 1921 and he traveled seeking a cure, she would accompany him, even aboard the house boat *Larooco*. She was accepted as one of the family by the Roosevelts. With Eleanor's blessing, she performed the duty of hostess for dinners and other social events during FDR's presidency. She called the president "F.D." and just like Louis Howe, she never backed down from telling Franklin her opinion on anything. Elliot Roosevelt quoted his father as saying, "Missy is my conscience."

FDR with friends from the *Larooco*, in 1924. Missy LeHand is on the left.

We have learned the simple truth, as Emerson said, that "The only way to have a friend is to be one."

—Fourth Inaugural Address, January 20, 1945

In the field of world policy, I would dedicate this Nation to the policy of the good neighbor; the neighbor who resolutely respects himself and, because he does so, respects the rights of others; the neighbor who respects his obligations and respects the sanctity of his agreements in and with a world of neighbors.

—First Inaugural Address, March 4, 1933

The noblest monument to peace and to neighborly economic and social friendship in all the world is not a monument in bronze or stone, but the boundary which unites the United States and Canada—3,000 miles of friendship with no barbed wire, no gun or soldier, and no passport on the whole frontier.

—Address at Chautauqua, New York, August 14, 1936

Fourteen years ago, a democratic Yankee, a comparatively young man, came to a neighboring county in the State of Georgia, came in search of a pool of warm water wherein he might swim his way back to health, and he found it. The place—Warm Springs—was at that time a rather dilapidated small summer resort. But his new neighbors there extended to him the hand of genuine hospitality, welcomed him to their firesides and made him feel so much at home that he built himself a house, bought himself a farm, and has been coming back ever since.

—Address at Barnesville, Georgia, August 11, 1938

*It is fun to be in the same
decade with you.*

—cable to Winston Churchill, December 1941

It is time that every citizen in
every one of the American republics
recognizes that the Good Neighbor
Policy means that harm to
one republic means harm to every
republic. We have all recognized the
principle of independence.
It is time we recognize the privilege
of interdependence—one
upon another.

—Address at Monterrey, Mexico, April 20, 1943

10

On Courage

On February 15, 1933, President-elect Franklin D. Roosevelt had just sat down in his open car after giving a speech at the Bayfront Park in Miami, when five shots rang out. Pandemonium followed as the Secret Service attacked a gunman only twenty-five feet from Roosevelt. As the gunfire erupted, Franklin sat firm, unbending to fear and awaiting anything fate would hand him. Miraculously he was uninjured, yet several people around him were not so lucky. Chicago mayor Anton Cermak lay mortally wounded in the stomach, and four others were also hit. As the driver hit the accelerator to escape the danger, Franklin ordered the car stopped to rescue Cermak. He could not have known if there were other assassins or if the crowd would become dangerous. Franklin would not rest until he had seen him settled in the hospital hours later. (Cermak did not survive.)

By any measure, this was a courageous act, yet Franklin's mettle had been tested in far greater ways as he fought over the

Franklin Roosevelt at Warm Springs in 1924.

Franklin and his mother, Sara, at Hyde Park in 1933.

years to recover from polio. There are other forms of courage, and for Franklin this meant everyday challenges to achieve greatness in the political limelight all the while being unable to walk. Frances Perkins recalled **FDR** speaking at a small public hall in New York City's Yorkville district on the campaign trail for the governorship of New York. The auditorium was crowded. The only entrance possible for him was up a small fire escape behind the stage. He could only arrive there through the willingness of strong men carrying him. "Those of us who saw this incident," she later wrote, "with our hands on our throats to hold down our emotion, realized that this man had accepted the ultimate humility which comes from being helped physically. He had accepted it smiling . . . For me and for others who saw that episode, his speech was less important than his courage . . . I began to see what the great teachers of religion meant when they said that humility is the greatest of virtues, and that if you can't learn it, God will teach it to you by humiliation. Only so, can a man be really great, and it was in those accommodations to necessity that Franklin Roosevelt began to approach the stature of humility and inner integrity which made him truly great."

> "I began to see what the great teachers of religion meant when they said that humility is the greatest of virtues, and that if you can't learn it, God will teach it to you by humiliation."
>
> —Frances Perkins

Franklin Roosevelt broadcasting his first fireside chat on March 12, 1933.

Confidence and courage are the essentials of success . . . . You people must have faith; you must not be stampeded by rumors or guesses.

—Fireside Chat, March 12, 1933

We have to have courage and discipline and vision to blaze the new trails in life; but underlying all our efforts is the conviction that men cannot live unto themselves alone. A democracy, the right kind of democracy, is bound together by the ties of neighborliness.

—Address to the National Conference of Catholic Charities, October 4, 1933

We in America know that our own democratic institutions can be preserved and made to work. But in order to preserve them we need to act together, to meet the problems of the nation boldly, and to prove that the practical operation of democratic government is equal to the task of protecting the security of the people.

—Fireside Chat, April 14, 1938

For a century and a half we have had here free education and a free press, free public forums, and a free pulpit. For more than a decade, we have had a free radio. The American citizen of 1936, therefore, is a product of free institutions. His mind has been sharpened by the exercise of freedom. That is why I have no fear either of the threats of demagogues or the ambitions of dictators. Neither can get far nor long thrive among a people who have learned to think for themselves and who have the courage to act as they think.

—Final Campaign Radio Speech of the 1936 Presidential Campaign, November 2, 1936

Eleanor, Franklin, and James Roosevelt enter the White House, March 4, 1933.

11

On Faith

Franklin Roosevelt's unshakable confidence was a hallmark of his leadership that endeared him to the American people. It was his Christian faith that gave him such strength. Raised as an Episcopalian, he had respect for all religions. Grace Tully, one of his secretaries who knew him for many years, said of him, "He believed in the efficacy of prayer and sought God's guidance in all the momentous decisions he was called on to make. He reaffirmed his faith in God in almost every speech he made as President." Franklin believed that America was a blessed country and that God had given him the strength to overcome his disability to lead when the country needed him. "He believed that Divine Providence had intervened to save him from total paralysis, despair, and death," noted Frances Perkins. "He saw the betterment of life and people a part of God's work, and he felt that man's devotion to God expressed itself by serving his fellow men."

James Roosevelt wrote about his father's faith in his own

memoirs: "In all the years I knew him, there was only one time when my father worried about his ability. It was the night he was elected president. I think the enormity of the power he had inherited struck him that night… Suddenly father found himself in control of his country, to a great extent responsible for the lives of many millions. I think he was concerned about the fact that he was, after all, a cripple, though he would not admit this worried him. We went back to our Manhattan home that night and talked alone. After a while, I helped him into bed and kissed him good-night.

"I am going to pray that God will help me, that He will give me the strength and the guidance to do this job and do it right."

He looked up at me and said, 'You know, Jimmy, all my life I have been afraid of one thing—fire. Tonight, I think I'm afraid of something else.'

"Afraid of what, father?" I asked.

'I'm just afraid that I may not have the strength to do the job. After you leave me tonight, Jimmy, I am going to pray. I am going to pray that God will help me, that He will give me the strength and the guidance to do this job and do it right.'"

Franklin sailing at Campobello in 1916

The only limit to our realization of tomorrow will be our doubts of today. Let us move forward with strong and active faith.

—Undelivered Address prepared for Jefferson Day, to be delivered April 13, 1945.

The Almighty God has blessed our
land in many ways. He has given our
people stout hearts and strong arms with
which to strike mighty blows for freedom
and truth. He has given to our country
a faith which has become the hope of all
peoples in an anguished world.
So we pray to Him now for the vision
to see our way clearly, to see the way that
leads to a better life for ourselves and
for all our fellow men, to the achievement
of His will to peace on earth.

—Fourth Inaugural Address, January 20, 1945

I am certain that out of the hearts of every man, woman, and child in this land, in every waking minute, a supplication goes up to Almighty God; that all of us beg that suffering and starving, that death and destruction may end—and that peace may return to the world. In common affection for all mankind, your prayers join with mine—that God will heal the wounds and the hearts of humanity.

—Fireside Chat, May 26, 1940

We do not see faith, hope, and charity as unattainable ideals, but we use them as stout supports of a nation fighting the fight for freedom in a modern civilization. Faith—in the soundness of democracy in the midst of dictatorships. Hope—renewed because we know so well the progress we have made. Charity—in the true spirit of that grand old word. For charity literally translated from the original means love, the love that understands, that does not merely share the wealth of the giver, but in true sympathy and wisdom helps men to help themselves.

—Speech to the Democratic National Convention, June 27, 1936

Today the whole world is divided between human slavery and human freedom — between pagan brutality and the Christian ideal. We choose human freedom — which is the Christian ideal.

—Fireside Chat, May 27, 1941

We have faith that future generations will know that here, in the middle of the twentieth century, there came a time when men of good will found a way to unite, and produce, and fight to destroy the forces of ignorance, and intolerance, and slavery, and war.

—Address to White House Correspondents Association, February 12, 1943

The supreme values are spiritual. The hope of the world is that character is built from the solid rock that withstands triumphantly the storms of life.

—Letter to the Chief of Chaplains of the War Department, February 13, 1934

12

Wisdom and Advice

Franklin Roosevelt possessed a mastery of the English language that had few equals among American presidents. Yet he knew the best way to reach the American people was to speak plainly, offering stories to exemplify his points. These became the heart of his fireside chat radio broadcasts that brought the president's voice and ideas into living rooms across the nation. "He developed the capacity to associate himself with great numbers of people," commented Frances Perkins. "He did not and could not know them all individually. He thought of them in family groups. He thought of them sitting around on a suburban porch after supper of a summer evening. He thought of them gathered around a dinner table at a family meal. He never thought of them as the masses. When he talked on the radio, he saw them gathered in the little parlor, listening with their neighbors. His voice and his facial expression as he spoke were those of an intimate friend."

Harvard senior portrait, 1904

Franklin and Eleanor with all thirteen of their grandchildren on January 20, 1945.

No man can tame a tiger into a kitten by stroking it.

—Arsenal of Democracy Speech, December 29, 1940